FLYING
and
OTHER STORIES
from the
OLD AND BOLD

FLYING
and
OTHER STORIES
from the
OLD AND BOLD

Compiled by John Daly, (RAF & RAAF) 1950-71

Contributors

Angus Cameron (World War 2)

Jim Flemming (USA exchange 1958)

Graham Neil (Malaysia 1960s)

Peter Larard (Vietnam 1960s)

Copyright © 2016 by John Daly.

ISBN:	Softcover	978-1-5245-1556-0
	eBook	978-1-5245-1555-3

All rights reserved. No part of this book may be reproduced or transmitted in any form or by any means, electronic or mechanical, including photocopying, recording, or by any information storage and retrieval system, without permission in writing from the copyright owner.

Any people depicted in stock imagery provided by Thinkstock are models, and such images are being used for illustrative purposes only.
Certain stock imagery © Thinkstock.

Print information available on the last page.

Rev. date: 08/02/2016

To order additional copies of this book, contact:
Xlibris
1-800-455-039
www.Xlibris.com.au
Orders@Xlibris.com.au
747284

TABLE OF CONTENTS

Chapter 1: Angus Cameron, Bomber Command, WW2 1

Chapter 2: Cranwell, 1952 and Tony Svensson 13

Chapter 3: Advanced Flying School Vampires to 3 Squadron Sabres 14

Chapter 4: Exercise Coronet and Armament Practice Camp Sylt 18

Chapter 5: Pilot Attack Course and Ginger Lacey, deployment to Cyprus 22

Chapter 6: Jim Flemming, on exchange to USA 25

Chapter 7: Staff OCU Chivenor, and HQ Fighter Command 28

Chapter 8: Graham Neil Malaysia 32

Chapter 9: Photo Recce, Middle East & Africa and RAAF 36

Chapter 10: Peter Larard, Vietnam 42

Chapter 11: Finale 56

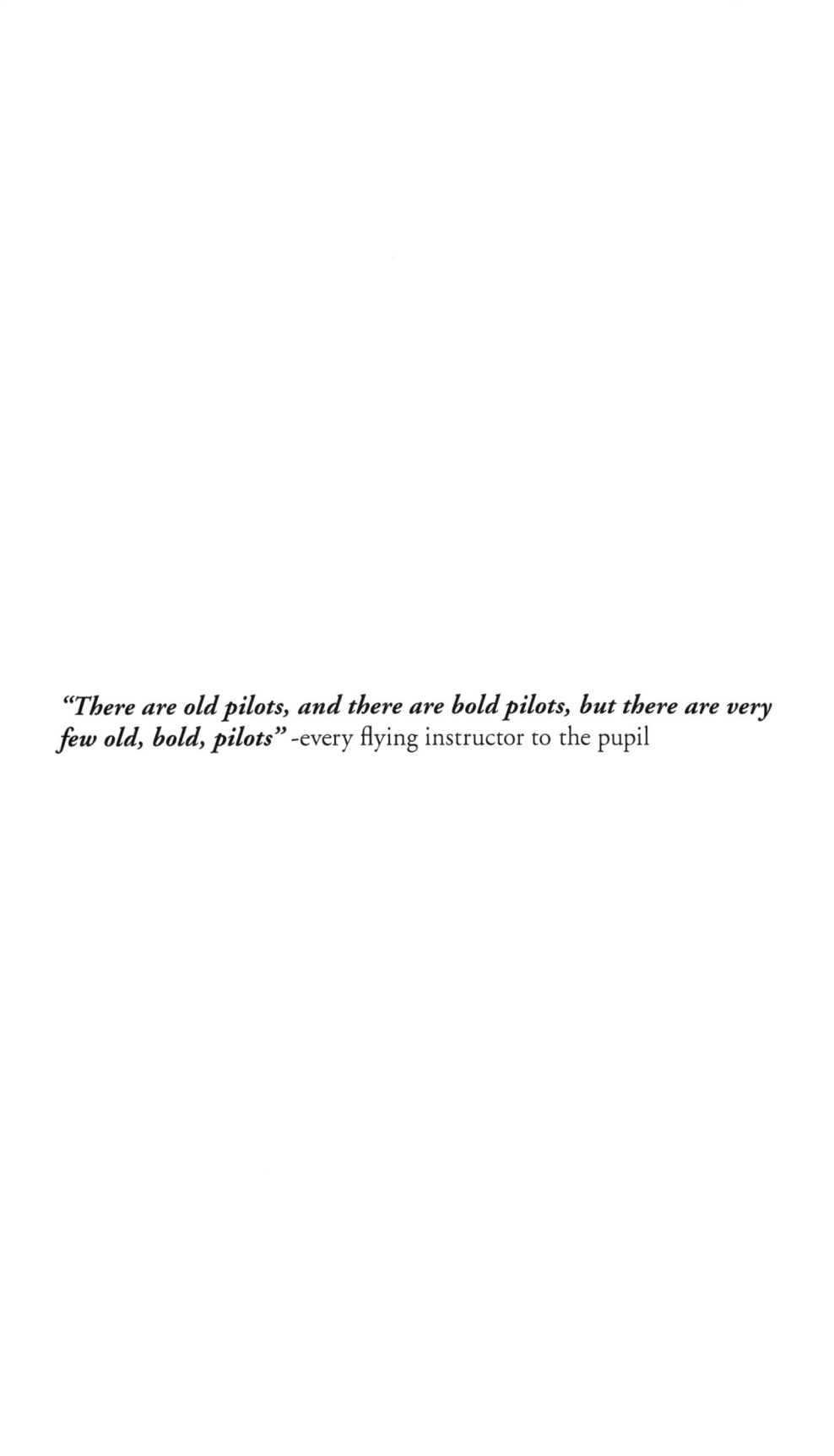

"There are old pilots, and there are bold pilots, but there are very few old, bold, pilots" -every flying instructor to the pupil

CHAPTER 1

I have been fortunate to have met some fascinating people in military aviation and either seen, experienced, or been told of (first hand), various exploits which people tell me deserve to be written down for others to enjoy. So this is not just my tale, but several others'. Whilst I never had to eject (unlike a friend who had no fewer than three departures from Hunters) nor had a major accident, I had a varied career and flew some fairly unusual aircraft with a few "interesting" experiences. I am truly grateful to some of my friends who have also contributed to this memoir. In chronological order the first of whom is

Angus Cameron (1944-45)

Angus was 91 when I met him in 2015. He was a great companion, as sharp as a tack, with completely clear recollections and a quick sense of humour. He had served in WW2 as a Wireless Operator in Bomber Command on special duties and completed 35 operations in his hazardous tour. I have always thought that as a group the aircrew of Bomber Command were the bravest people in the war; to go off night after night to be shot at for 7 hours or so, with appalling casualty rates, required the most tremendous courage. Just imagine being shot up, limping home under constant attack, finally making it over the Dover cliffs, heaving a sigh of relief and wonderment that you have survived - and then going off a few days later to do it all again. And again. And again. Angus' task was even more dangerous than normal bombers', since his job was to stay longer on target attracting attention. The statistics at the end of his piece are dreadful. Angus described to me how the "mon dieu" cries of alarm got louder and more frequent from his Belgian pilot/captain when particularly close anti-aircraft explosions or particularly pressing fighter attacks were striking his aircraft! Angus started with a crew of 5 in Wellingtons and kept with the same crew (of which more later) throughout, other than the navigator who was replaced. Additions were made as the aircraft got bigger until they had 10 for their later operations. I persuaded him to let me have his memoir and here it is:-

"On 11 July 1944 we arrived at No 1657 Heavy Conversion Unit, RAF Stradishall, Suffolk, where we were to be introduced to four-engined bombers. To operate these aircraft a Flight Engineer had to be added to the crew; ours was a Scotsman. Our new aircraft were Stirlings, which were truly large, but suffered from an inability to operate at very great heights with a full load. They also had some interesting handling deficiencies, on take-off in particular, but our skipper soon mastered these huge aeroplanes and by the time we left Shepherd's Grove (our satellite airfield) at the end of August we were assessed as being ready to go to a bomber squadron.

Instead of being posted to a Lancaster or Halifax squadron as we had expected, we went to RAF Base Oulton, (13 miles NNW of Norwich, Norfolk), to join No 214 (FMS) SD Squadron, a unit of No 100 (Bomber Support) Group, Bomber Command. Group Headquarters was located at Bylaugh Hall, about 10 miles west of Oulton. FMS stood for Federated Malay States, because in September 1941 the Squadron was honoured by being officially "adopted" by the British Malayan Federation; SD stood for Special Duties, and we were more than a little intrigued about how special our duties were going to be!

The biggest surprise was the type of aircraft we were to use: American Boeing B17s. 214 Sqn was the only squadron in Bomber Command to use these "Flying Fortresses", although some earlier models had been used by RAF bomber squadrons in the first years of the war while awaiting the development of Lancaster-type aircraft. At Oulton was located the squadron's own conversion unit, No 1699 Heavy Conversion Unit, where we started our training on 9 September 1944. The step up from Stirlings to Fortresses was of course less time-consuming, although we all had to learn about our new US equipment, including a radio installation I had never heard of!

We suffered a slight setback when we had the misfortune, through a landing gear failure on touchdown, to crash on landing one night, virtually destroying the aircraft, but we all pressed on despite some injuries that in my case have come back to give me some problems. The course concluded with a "Bullseye" - a night "attack" on London - and having graduated, we moved across to join 214 Sqn proper.

The most immediate change in our lives from this point on was that we now found ourselves awaiting advice each morning (or afternoon) as to whether our crew was on the "battle order" - if we were, we had to set-to preparing ourselves for the operational flight planned for that night, not knowing the name of the target until briefing time an hour or two before take-off. While waiting for the briefing, there were many things to do: go out to the allotted aircraft, parked in one of the dispersal areas, and check our respective equipment, (in my case the radio and associated equipment), ensure that guns were serviceable and ammunition taken aboard and so on. In most cases a short "NFT" (a night flying test) flight was undertaken, just to ensure that the engines all worked and the aircraft was in good shape for the coming "op". We could not test our radios at that time as the enemy constantly was "listening out" to detect signs of activity which could give them warning of impending operations.

The squadron had been equipped with B17 Fortress aircraft because they could fly significantly higher than the other RAF bombers, and they had heavier defensive armament, which were two important attributes required for the squadron's special role. As we discovered, they could also survive well after sustaining severe damage, both to engines (which were in any case very reliable) and airframes (which were extremely well-made). On the negative side they were slow (155 knots, even when coming home) and could not carry a great payload. To carry out our specialised duties in these aircraft we had expanded our crew from seven to ten: two air gunners were added, one from Wales and the other from Chester, plus a German-speaking special radio officer (another Australian).

The gunners operated the waist guns, standing at large openings cut in each side of the aircraft, through which came a howling, cold and very noisy blast of air. At operational height the two waist gunners, and the tail gunner, all looked like snowmen, being covered in frost, and of course the cold air penetrated throughout the aircraft. The whole crew combated the cold, often about minus 30 degrees C, by wearing electrically-heated flying suits, with gloves and fleecy-lined boots, but we suffered microphone problems because the mechanical parts would freeze solid, and constant freeing-up was required to ensure that ever-important messages could be exchanged clearly and quickly between all the crew members. Unlike the crews often shown in the movies we did not carry any weapons on our person.

Our crew consisted of (with ranks and ages in April 1945 when we completed our operational tour): Pilot and Captain (Skipper) - Flight Lieutenant Marc Stainier, about 32 years, RAF (Belgium); Navigator - Flying Officer Basil Coates, about 26 years, RAAF, replaced during our tour as Navigator by Flying Officer John Wallace, about 25 years, RCAF; Bomb-Aimer/Radar Operator, back-up navigator, emergency (untrained) pilot and expert map-reader - Warrant Officer Phil Troutbeck, about 28 years, RAAF; Flight Engineer - Sergeant Jim Lando, about 19 years, RAF (Scotland); Wireless Operator (and back-up air-gunner, if desperate) - Warrant Officer Angus Cameron, 20 years, RAAF; Special Radio Officer - Flying Officer Charles Miflin, about 28 years, RAAF; Mid-Upper Gunner - Sergeant Jim Scott, about 19 years, RAF (Scotland); Waist Gunner - Sergeant Bill Walsh, about 20 years, RAF (Cheshire); Waist Gunner - Sergeant "Taffy" Williams, about 30 years, RAF (Wales); Rear Gunner - Sergeant Don Hatch, about 21 years, RAF (Southampton).

We now learned our role: two special types of duties were carried out by the squadron, sometimes one at a time and sometimes combined. The first role was to disrupt German fighter-control radio transmissions, and the second was to disrupt all manner of German defensive radars.

The disruption of their radio networks was carried out by carrying high-powered radio transmitters in our aircraft, and either jamming the enemy's transmissions or broadcasting conflicting instructions, in

German, to the Luftwaffe fighter pilots being directed towards the attacking RAF bombers. Details of the German radio frequencies we were to interfere with were progressively radioed to us from England where they were continually being monitored as we penetrated further into the Third Reich, and as the German fighter control system alerted its squadrons to intercept us.

The special radio man sat across the aircraft from me, with his consoles in front of him, his transmitters being located in the bomb-bay, which was virtually filled with electronic gear. When he found a German frequency in use to direct the fighters from the ground, he would quickly match it on his dials and then transmit a powerful jamming signal which, being sent out from so close to the German fighters, would force the enemy to change to another channel. Our man would then start searching for the new frequency; at the same time it was often possible for the monitoring people back in England to quickly detect the new frequency and transmit it in code to me, which I would decode and hand across to our operator.

He would then either repeat the jamming exercise or, if he felt ambitious interrupt their transmissions and pretend to be the German controller. When they were interrupted, their reaction was always spectacular; if they were being jammed with noise they would change frequency as quickly as possible, clearly expressing their frustration when they resumed contact with their fighters. On those occasions when they had to contend with our man's (Australian-accented) German language, the controllers would shout to the fighter aircraft under their control to "ignore the Englishman" (sic) and then our operator would try and convince them that he in fact was the real controller. Not often would they wholly swallow the story but they **were** confused, and angry, and no doubt their efficiency was reduced, even if only to the extent that they would spend time trying to "home" in on the radio transmissions from our equipment, both voice and noise, and destroy us. As our jamming equipment was gradually refined and improved, the need to resort to voice transmissions diminished, but we remained very vulnerable to detection and attack by the enemy fighters.

To perform this countermeasures function we were required to accompany the Bomber Command Pathfinders (or other lead-aircraft) to the target, ahead of the main force, and after the initial marker flares had been laid, we would orbit the target and transmit our jamming and/or false fighter control instructions, meanwhile dispensing "window" - paper-backed metal foil strips - which were designed to confuse the German radars: these included early-warning and fighter control radars as well as searchlight control and anti-aircraft gun control radars. We would then continue our orbiting, usually several thousand feet above the Lancasters and Halifaxes as they progressively arrived and made their attacks.

When the raid was completed, or we were relieved by another Fortress, we would head for home. Because we had been transmitting, and "windowing", furiously over the target for something like fifteen minutes each time, we automatically became objects of great interest to the German radio countermeasures people, who had little difficulty hearing and locating our transmitters, and then directing their fighters and/or anti-aircraft guns on to us.

Our aircraft could reach upwards of 30,000 feet in altitude, which was helpful in avoiding both fighters and guns, although they managed to reach us on enough occasions to do damage to our aircraft but thankfully not to ourselves. Our .50" calibre Browning machine guns were heavier than the .303" guns in the Lancasters & Halifaxes, (although we only had six of them), and we were able to put up a spirited defence when attacked. Like all night bombers we maintained a weaving pattern when over enemy territory, in order to make us a more difficult target, although this sometimes brought us into uncomfortably close proximity to unseen friendly aircraft doing exactly the same thing.

To aid our gunners, we had a tail-attack warning radar, called Monica, which had its small monitor screen located on my radio table; when I detected a "blip" closing in behind us, I would warn our gunners, give them its range and direction, and they would then look for it, which was difficult in the dark. If and when the fighter was sighted the gunners would instruct the skipper to "corkscrew (up or down, left or right, as appropriate) - NOW", whereupon the pilot would for example dive the aircraft sharply, while turning at the same time. He would then roll the other way and climb, repeating this as long as was necessary to make it difficult for the swifter fighters to aim and fire, while our gunners fired back as fiercely as they could; not an easy thing to do as we corkscrewed through the air. This was where all that air-to-air training at OTU paid dividends. While these manoeuvres were going on it was difficult to know our exact position, or for that matter which way up we were.

Considering that these chases were occurring in the dark, changing height and direction at speed while surrounded by perhaps 50 or 100 other (mostly friendly) aircraft, not visible and heading in all directions at that stage of the attack, it was remarkable that we did not suffer the fate of the 50% of crews - yes, one in every two - who did not survive Bomber Command operations. After we left the target our biggest problem was then to return to Base, sometimes 3 to 4 hours away, without sustaining further attacks and damage. To her credit the B17 aircraft could fly well on fewer than 4 engines and we managed to return on several occasions with 3, sometimes 2 and once (for a time) on one engine. The cliffs of Old England, in the dawn light, were a very welcome sight under those circumstances.

Our other role involved a highly developed "spoof" technique. On most occasions when an enemy target was to be attacked, a second (or even a third or fourth) force would be despatched at the same time as the main force, with the object of putting doubt into the mind of the Germans as to which was the main target and which was a diversion. At suitable points along their path the various groups of aircraft would divide, and perhaps repeat the division further along, so that often the Luftwaffe would commit its main fighter forces to the wrong stream of attacking aircraft. On these missions we carried a heavy load of "window", of the appropriate length and width to simulate convincing echoes on the German radars, and which we dispensed at carefully measured rates.

On occasions, only a few, (typically three) Fortresses would be used in a particular feint, thereby drawing much of the Luftwaffe onto us, at least until the wider plot emerged on their radar screens; these in particular were exciting times! In addition to their important gunnery role, the waist gunners had the task of opening the large bundles of "window" and dispensing the appropriate number of strips at a predetermined rate through a chute in the floor; at least it helped them keep warm. When we were carrying out a corkscrew manoeuvre, the large bundles of bulk "window", each weighing upwards of 110 lbs, had a habit of migrating about the fuselage, much to everyone's dismay.

Throughout each operational flight my role was to maintain a continuous listening watch on my radio equipment, for it was essential that I heard and acted on **all** Morse messages from England, either addressed directly to us or as part of "general broadcasts" intended for all aircraft taking part in the raid. The consequences of missing a message intended for you could be disastrous if for example, all aircraft were recalled or re-directed to a different target because of deteriorating weather over Germany; one lonely aircraft could end up as an easy victim for the German defences.

Because I was "listening out" all the time, and concentrating hard to distinguish the weak radio signals under poor receiving conditions, I was switched off from the main intercom conversations, except when I was specifically spoken to or needed to speak to the skipper or other crew member. As a result it was sometimes hard to stay switched off when the aircraft was going through all manner of evasive manoeuvres, and I could see the strong beams of the searchlights and hear the noise and feel the impact of flak; if my curiosity (or apprehension) drove me to listen in to the rest of the crew, I was usually only too glad to switch back to my "radio world" because everyone seemed to be speaking at once!

My other role of course was to contact Base or other radio stations, to pass on important messages or to obtain bearings or fixes to help our navigator; this role was strictly governed by the need to maintain radio silence unless it was absolutely necessary to touch the Morse key. Nevertheless, we obviously were able to work well together, and managed to solve each problem as it arose.

Through that autumn and winter we flew 35 operational (i.e. against the enemy) sorties, which started with five to Holland, Denmark, and the Frisian Islands and then 30 sorties into the Third Reich: Heligoland,

Essen, Coblenz (twice), Cologne (twice), the Ruhr area, Munster, Duisburg (three times), Osnabruck, Mannheim, Munchen Gladbach (twice), Dortmund, Karlsruhe (twice), Politz (9 hrs 40 mins, just about maximum endurance of the aircraft), Mainz, Bonn, Chemnitz (7 hrs 30 mins), Leipzig (7 hrs 40 mins), Dusseldorf (twice), Kassel, Bohlen-Leipzig (8 hrs 50 mins), Kiel, Bremerhaven, and Hamburg. These amounted to 194 hours 35 minutes night flying against the enemy, and completed my operational tour.

Our original crew remained intact to the end, except a replacement Navigator was acquired about midway through; he was from Canada, thus reducing the number of Australians to three, but proved to be a fine crew member.

As we had completed our tour, and there were then encouraging signs that the war against Germany was coming to a close, we were sent on leave in mid-April 1945, with instructions to await a telegram regarding our future postings, either as a crew or individually. We Australians had been put on notice that a force called "Tiger Force" was now being planned, with the object of transferring experienced aircrew members and suitable aircraft (including the newly-developed, "tropicalised", version of the Lancaster) to the Pacific to finish-off the Japanese.

In our fatalistic way we went on leave, I to London of course, and awaited the anticipated telegram. Thankfully, the leave was extended and I was able to catch up on some long-overdue medical treatment for some flying-caused ailments. Eventually, VE-Day came and the war in Europe ended and I realised that our crew had finally been broken up! I was posted on 12 July 1945 to No 9 Aircrew Holding Unit, RAF Gamston, Nottinghamshire, "for disposal".

Instead of the expected call forward to the Pacific, we were told we would be progressively repatriated, as soon as the required troopships could be found. Since there were so many Australians awaiting transport, we were again sent on leave, to await the now familiar telegram. When it came (I think about late September), I found myself on a troop train to Southampton, and was overjoyed to see the black-painted Orient ship ORION awaiting us. On boarding the ship, however, we were dismayed to find the accommodation provided consisted of trestle tables deep in the hold, with hammocks strung above; this was completely unsatisfactory from a health aspect for a protracted journey through the tropics. To our own surprise, and even more so to the British Army transport organisers, we walked off the ship immediately and assembled on the wharf. There were some 400 of us, mostly experienced aircrew, and we felt - to a man - that such treatment was beyond a joke. After some discussion with the OC Troops (who suggested that we were some sort of mutineers!), we were told to wait, and eventually a train came in, carrying young British Army troops, posted to Italy for garrison duty. They boarded the ship in our place, and she sailed, still carrying our kitbags and paybooks, which the OC Troops insisted was done to teach us a lesson!

We then went in the train, kitless, and payless, to 11 PDRC Brighton, where we were paraded, spoken to severely by the RAAF Air Vice-Marshal, and then sent on leave! Since we had little money, we soon found employment in London: as "extras" on the set for the film "Caesar and Cleopatra", and more enjoyable (but less lucrative) employment by Watney Combe & Reid, then the largest Brewery in London. Ironically, the ORION broke down, (we were not surprised), and returned to England, and we were reunited with our kit and paybooks.

At last we were forgiven, and I boarded the DURBAN CASTLE on 21 December 1945, and arrived in Sydney 21 January 1946. After processing at No 2 Personnel Depot RAAF Bradfield Park, an understandably slow process at that stage of the war, I was discharged on 13 March 1946 - just three years & five months after I first put on RAAF uniform. I was 21 years old.

Post Script: The last page of my Flying Log Book contains a certificate which reads:

Air Officer Commanding No 100 Group Commendation on

Completion of Operational Tour:

**Aus 429007 Warrant Officer AL CAMERON
RAAF No 214 Squadron.**

"For Meritorious Service and good airmanship, in that a full operational tour has been completed without having been involved in any accident or ever having an unnecessary cancellation or abandonment of an operational sortie."

Signed : RE CHISHOLM Air Commodore RAF

for Air Vice-Marshal,

Air Officer Commanding

In a book published by Air Commodore Chisholm in 1953 titled "Cover of Darkness", (Chatto and Windus) he wrote, Quote: "...our hope in interfering with German radio broadcasts, combined with selective use of "window", was to delay the enemy's understanding of the bomber plan and to gain for the main force at least another few minutes' immunity from interception. The enemy fighters, even if the jamming of their radio was severe, were still dangerous, for they would see the opening of an attack from afar and some would be able to reach it before the bombing had finished. Once there, the more experienced among them could pick out the bombers in the glare of the fires or from a chance sighting of exhausts or with their radar, the efficiency of which might have been reduced but not nullified by jamming." Unquote.

We (214 Sqn) were particularly vulnerable, in that we tended to invite attention at a time when it was helpful to be as inconspicuous as possible: depending on our specified task we either had to remain in the target area for a prolonged period (much longer than the attacking bombers which came, and went), all the while transmitting signals on which the enemy fighters could very easily "home"; or we sailed along deliberately putting out "window" which was after all designed to be detected! Chisholm continues in his book, Quote: **"These 'spoof' forces were the scapegoats for the bombing forces.** The hard fact was that if the plan was to succeed completely, and if the attention of all the enemy fighters was diverted from the main force or forces to the "spoof" force and the latter suffered even total loss, the loss would have been justified because the fighter opportunities would have been limited to the smaller number of aircraft of the "spoof" force, while the much larger number of main attack aircraft would remain unscathed. **These "spoofs", although some of the least known, were perhaps among the finest operations of the air war."** Unquote.

This view was reinforced in 1955 by Luftwaffe General of the Fighters Adolf Galland, in his book "The First & the Last" (Methuen) p337, Quote:" There was no shortage of night fighter aircraft. From the middle of 1944 onwards the Luftwaffe could even speak of a surplus. The decrease of the German night fighter successes in this period was mainly due to interference, shortage of fuel, **and the activities of the RAF No 100 Group**. The task of this special unit was to mislead our fighters and to befog our conception of the air situation by clever deceptive manoeuvres. This specialist unit finally solved its task so well that it was hardly ever absent from any of the British night operations, and it can claim to have set really difficult problems for the German night fighter command." Unquote.

FOOTNOTE STATISTIC: From Australia's point of view, while just 2% of all Australian servicemen served in Bomber Command, their losses represented 20% of all Australian service combat deaths."

Comments by Daly: I asked Angus how it was he became a Warrant Officer at the age of 20; normally achieved much later in life, being the peak of the non-commissioned officers rank structure. He told me that during the war the RAAF gave promotions to operational aircrew based on time; after six months as Sergeant they were made up to Flight Sergeant and a further six months later Warrant Officer. This caused some angst with their RAF equivalents, who were not given such a generous arrangement. I also asked why they did 35 ops instead of the normal 30; he said it was originally 30 and it was changed by "someone in the Air Ministry" to 35 just when they had completed 29. Further, owing to weather etc the last six took several months with their final op being flown on a Friday 13th The navigator who was replaced suffered from shell-shock; on a particularly hazardous trip, returning home with a great deal of damage, he suddenly put down his pencil and said "I can't do this any more". Another crew member acted as nav the rest of the way home.

CHAPTER 2

I was trained on Prentices and Harvards at RAF College Cranwell - two and a half years' slog in which we only got about 220 hours flying. My tale is of

Tony Svensson (1952)

I was on the same course as Tony; towards the end our flying instructors organised a spot landing competition. We were taken to a nearby field, where they marked a square in white on the grass. We were each to close the throttle on our Harvards at 1500 feet and perform a glide approach, landing as near as possible or preferably on the white marker without any application of throttle, which would of course be heard. However we Flight Cadets also got together and agreed we'd have our own competition (unbeknown to staff, of course) for the most spectacular take-off.

Harvards had retractable undercarriages and the instructors were appalled as we all in turn flew really low down and failed to climb away till the last minute, however Tony took the cake; he knew the sequence in which the undercarriage was raised, and that it was monitored by a switch on each leg. Tony achieved flying speed and slightly raised the right wing, leaving some weight on the left wheel; he then raised the undercarriage, the right wheel came up and Tony "flew" for about 70 yards with one wheel firmly on the ground. He also won the spot landing and subsequently the College Flying prize! Later he was known as the test pilot who suffered terrible injuries resulting from a supersonic ejection from a Mirage in Australia.

CHAPTER 3

I have a recollection which still makes me quiver with fear. After graduating from Cranwell I was sent to RAF Valley on the Isle of Anglesea to convert onto Vampires, then front-line fighters. The course incorporated a helicopter rescue practice from the sea, which we all completed. One day I was last to land and the transport up to the Mess had already gone, leaving me with a walk of over a mile. As I trudged along a chopper flew by and I jokingly waved a thumb as though hitching a lift. To my delight down came a strop, so I put it on and indicated I was ready in the approved manner.

Up I was winched, but the chopper went higher and higher to what I estimate to be 3000 feet, simultaneously letting out the winch cable to its full length, so I was dangling far below; then the bastards did a couple of short sideways movements and I was swinging on a very long pendulum some 2000 feet above the ground. I was terrified, hanging on for dear life, feeling physically sick from fear. The thought of it still gives me shivers.

After OCU on Vampires at Chivenor, I was finally posted to Germany where I asked for and got all 3 of my choices – 3 Squadron who were to be the first Sabre Squadron and was part of Johnnie (JEJ) Johnson's wing at Wildenrath. The introduction of the new generation of fighters had been hastened by the Korean War. The RAF was still awaiting the British Hawker Hunter, but the Russian MIG 15 was already in service. Hence the RAF had to order Sabres in order to fill the gap. However for the time being we had Vampires; very basic little aircraft with no navigation aids at all and no ejector seat. Even in Vampires we spent quite a lot of time on "the unmentionable" i.e. Battle Flight, where we were the first line of defence against any Russian aggression. This involved sitting in the cockpit of a fully armed aircraft at the end of the runway, ready to "scramble" i.e. take-off, to intercept well-armed, high speed Soviet bombers at a moment's notice. This was taking place as they say nowadays "24/7" – that is every day and night, including Christmas. The Russians occasionally would test our state of preparedness by flying up to the border and our radar guys would scramble us. On wet cold days it was pretty miserable, but I was so lucky not to be on Night All-Weather fighter duties (NF Meteors at that time, later Javelins). NAW fighters had intercept radar and carried a navigator to operate it. Those poor souls not only had to do this when the weather was too bad for us but sometimes had to go off into snow and storms in the dark. I believe there were many pilots who really did not want to do that, but just gritted their teeth and did their duty.

After I spent a few months on Vampires 3 Squadron was indeed the first to convert to Sabres, the RAF's first swept-wing aircraft, and pretty proud we were! However conversion to this new generation fighter included ground school, where we were introduced to the mysteries of hydraulic powered controls, radar ranging gun-sight, American ejector seat and a radio compass – this last a most useful navigation aid, not only did it point to the radio station selected – commercial or military base - but by mental arithmetic (at which we got better very quickly) allowed one to calculate one's position by the rate at which the pointer changed direction. It also allowed one to listen to music whilst on the unmentionable.

However our first task, really even as we were converting, was to take part in the Queen's Coronation Review on 15 July 1953. JEJ's wing of 3 and 67 Squadrons flew our Sabres to Duxford in Cambridgeshire and operated from there for this operation. Some 630 aircraft took part in the flypast, formations passing the Royal Dais at precisely 30 second intervals. Slowest aircraft first. Rehearsals and careful flight planning and timing ensured all went well. Impressive – but the scene 10 miles past, where everybody caught each other up, was a sight to see! Being the only swept wing guys and the fastest aircraft in Service, we went last – except for, as the Times put it "and finally came a lone Hawker Hunter, flown, or rather aimed, by Mr Neville Duke".

The Queen was positioned at RAF Odiham in Southern England for the fly past, which was commanded by Paddy Bandon who was in attendance upon the Queen. There was a static display there too, with an example of every sort of aircraft positioned for review. I was detailed to go to the depot and collect a Sabre and deliver it for the display; the first time most of our people had seen one of this new-generation fighter was my taxiing in and so it caused considerable interest. My ex-Squadron Commander from Cranwell was in charge of the static display. He had not liked me and had made it plain – and he it was who met my Sabre and greeted me; he was plainly shocked when I took off my oxygen mask and he identified the pilot! A great pleasure it was, to see his discomfiture.

Soon after we returned to Wildenrath, the Squadron was re-deployed to a new base nearby called Geilenkirchen. As all we knew was close formation, our inexperienced Squadron Commander (he had been an officer in the Tank Regiment and transferred to the RAF keeping the same rank) decided we would do a close formation fly past at 2000 feet over our new base to announce our arrival. We had 16 aircraft so had a "box" of four boxes of four and as I was still the junior pilot I was in the "slot" of the rear four. We took off and quickly were into formation. With 81% power set we should have about 320 knots airspeed, ideal and what we had been used to. Our valiant leader though had about 85% set, which increased the speed somewhat. There were big thunderstorms about and sure enough one right over our route to Geilenkirchen, with the cloud lowering. Approaching Geilenkirchen we were forced lower and lower to stay under the cloud and this descent increased our speed further to around 470 knots; suddenly we were in a really thick black cloud, which was very turbulent. I was also getting near the ground, being at the back and lowest. At this point our gallant leader called "Airbrakes, GO". The Sabre at high speed would give a violent nose up movement on application of airbrakes and it would have taken greater experience than we had to maintain formation in those conditions. The air was thick with aircraft breaking off formation with pilots going straight onto instrument flying, close to the ground, in close proximity to 15 other aircraft and in heavy turbulence. My good fortune was that I knew no one was behind me, so I closed my throttle completely as I popped the airbrakes: also I could see the ground, and remained visual. Amazingly there were no collisions, but instead of an impressive flypast we arrived at our new base somewhat ignominiously as sixteen individual aircraft.

CHAPTER 4

Exercise Coronet, the last of the great air exercises, was held in Germany in 1953, shortly after our arrival at Geilenkirchen. Total realism except for live rounds, it had 2nd TAF (British, Dutch and Belgian Air Forces) against USAF. The reason it was the last is because it was so expensive, some 26 aircraft destroyed and I believe 7 pilots killed. Held in midsummer it was a daylight only affair, but we had to get up at 2.30 to be on alert at the end of the runway by 3.30 and we could not leave the flight line until 9.45 at night. Since we had as many aircraft (F86 Sabres) as we did pilots there was no opportunity for a break. After five days of this we were all pretty tired, after a week I suspect dangerous. Flat out from take-off to landing and mostly at very low level we ran short of fuel very quickly (about 20 minutes). I personally diverted into another airfield when I realised how short I was: the engine stopped for lack of fuel as I turned off the runway and I had to call for a tractor to tow me to the flight line.

I was not surprised when I heard 2 of ours returning to Geilenkirchen very short of fuel from different directions and they told the tower they would land simultaneously in opposite directions on our single runway. One of the pilots said to the other "You keep left and I'll keep right" there was a short pause and then a yell of "NO - WE BOTH KEEP LEFT"; luckily he was not too tired to concur with the first suggestion, because I believe I would have been sucked in. As it was it was pretty spectacular, passing each other about mid point.

In the same exercise one of the Wildenrath chaps was going down a valley in his Vampire when he flew into someone coming the other way. He discovered that though he was missing most of his left wing, he could sort of control the aircraft as long as he was going faster than 260 knots. So he went back to Wildenrath and put it down on the very beginning of the 2,700 yard runway, wheels up of course. Bits flew off as he slid down the runway until there was virtually nothing left. He used up the whole runway's length, with a bit of debris on every yard. Luckily in the Vampire the pilot's seat is directly above the guns, which were considerably worn down (or up) and when he came to a stop the pilot simply undid his straps and stepped forward out of the seat!

During another exercise a month or two later I was flying as wing man to a very experienced Sergeant Pilot, Ken (the Baron) Chapple, in a formation of 12 climbing south. At about 32,000 feet Ken drifted out of formation across me and the leader told me to stay with him, which I did staying in battle formation about 50 yards away. Ken did not answer my calls but his aircraft swung round and down. Suddenly it blew up and I called "he's exploded". Nowadays there are many photos of aircraft transitioning from sub to supersonic, with massive shock waves coming off the whole airplane, but none of us had seen such a thing. However I quickly realised that the "explosion" was him going through the sound barrier as I went supersonic too. I guess I was probably one of the first to see it at close hand and Ken was certainly the first to "go through" unconscious and live. As we came to a lower altitude his aircraft levelled out and eventually he regained consciousness and control, responded to my calls and followed me back to base. Later, after a cup of coffee, he came up and quietly said "Thank you, John".

Tempests. In 1946, aged 17 I went to Germany to spend Christmas with my mother, who was then manager of the Malcolm Club (a welfare organisation for the RAF) at RAF Wunstdorf. I became friends with one of the "Malcy" girls, Sylvia, who was becoming engaged to Reg Merchant, a Flying Officer on 3 Squadron stationed there. Reg kindly invited me down to the Squadron, who were flying Tempests. Reg and Sylvia became my life-long friends. I thought the world of 3 Squadron and so admired the whole set-up that I promised myself I would get on to 3 Sqn and to fly these magnificent aircraft and as you see, I had achieved the first ambition.

In the 1950s Fighter Squadrons in Germany would go about once a year for APC (Armament Practice Camp) at Sylt, an airfield right on the Danish border, for live firing at banners towed over the sea. On the other side of the airfield at Sylt there was a special Target Towing flight, whose boring task was to tow the targets for visiting Squadrons to shoot at. This flight was manned by pretty gung-ho pilots who were being punished, usually for some fairly major indiscretion; it was administratively difficult to send these people back to the UK, so target towing was a compromise punishment. The flight operated Tempests. Mindful of my time eight years previously, I went over to the Target Towing flight and introduced myself as from the visiting Sabre Squadron (the first they'd seen) and asked if there was any chance I could have a fly of one of their Tempests. The flight commander, having established the fact the last piston aircraft I had flown was a Harvard, said "OK" and gave me a copy of Pilot's Notes to read. To my horror, about 5 minutes later I had got to about page 3 when he came into the crew-room and said "All right, off we go then", authorised me in the book and led me out to the aircraft.

I climbed into this huge beast. The first thing I noticed was I could not see anything outside; I was accustomed to a good view from jets but in the Tempest the enormous engine was tilted up before me, so the large propeller in front was clear of the ground. The Flight Lieutenant leaned in and started it for me, told me to wait until the temperatures were OK before going. His final words were "watch the swing on take-off" – but he did not say which way!

The monster shook and made a mighty noise; I did not know what speed to climb at, nor anything else. I realised I had been extremely foolish and that I would most likely kill myself on this stupid venture. Nevertheless I could not possibly back down; my plan was, if I survived take-off, to climb to a reasonable height and do some stalls to establish a landing speed. So when it had warmed up I called for taxi clearance, was given it, waved chocks away and stated taxiing forward. I had moved about a yard when the marshalling airman suddenly gave the stop sign;

he climbed up to the cockpit and yelled "Hydraulic Leak". I then had to ask him how to turn the engine off. I carried the parachute back to the flight office, explained how sad I was at the unserviceability and departed for sanity on my side of the airfield. No I never went back and to this day I do not know if they did that to all their visitors, or whether the leak was genuine, or whether it was all just a tease.

CHAPTER 5

In 1955 I was sent to the PAI (Pilot Attack Instructor) course at the Central Gunnery School at Leconfield. Instead of Sabres I suddenly was on Meteor 8s for cine and air to air, and Venom 4s for dive-bombing, rockets and air to ground. No there was no conversion – just get in them and fly! Most attendees were from meteor squadrons, but I just climbed into a Meteor for a "famil" flight, in my case both the aircraft and the local area. After that - onto the range. How times change. Meteors were enjoyable to fly, though the RAF lost 890 of them in service, resulting in the death of 450 pilots. The Venoms I thought wonderful – a sort of super Vampire with a good ejector seat, they had plenty of power (you could loop them at 40,000 feet) were highly manoeuvrable and a steady gun platform. Also the course was very enjoyable and I did quite well, but a highlight was meeting

Ginger Lacey

Ginger was I believe the second highest scoring British fighter ace (after JEJ) in WW2. There is a long screed on him in Wikipedia. Ginge was posted there as a sort of mascot – a great guy, brave etc but not truly instructor material (lousy shot on the banner) but excellent in the bar! He told us some tales about pre-war flying, when he would be hired to take press photographers around and one occasion was when the submarine Thetis, which had sunk near Liverpool in 1939 with heavy loss of life, was to be brought to the surface by a salvage team. This was keenly anticipated and several aircraft were buzzing round the salvage vessel in circles, but the sub did not come up. Gradually the weather closed in and the aircraft left, one by one, till only Ginger was there. And up came the sub! The photographer, wildly excited, took his photos and urged Ginger to fly direct to London. He also pointed out that as they had an "exclusive" they were each on a big bonus. The weather had become extremely poor and Ginger pointed out that there was a mountain called Snowdon in the way, so it was necessary to cross to the East side of England and find a railway line to London. Whilst following this line (pretty standard practice in those days) they saw 2 trains approaching each other and right in front of them there was a major train smash! Another exclusive and bonus.

On another press trip several aircraft were buzzing around trying to get pictures of the German Fleet moving through the Channel. Once again on the point of giving up Ginger, in very low visibility, to quote his words "nearly rammed the Gneisenau amidships". Yet another exclusive.

We found his log book for the Battle of Britain time. I remember seeing several "shot down Ju 88" and "shot down Me 110", but also several "shot down by 109". He was I believe shot down 4 times. Finally there was "shot down 109" and in huge letters on the right page he had written "SUCCESS AT LAST!"

After my PAI course, in 1955 the Squadron was sent to Cyprus for APC – probably because Sylt was fully booked and the weather factor allowed much more flying in Cyprus. With the very short range of the aircraft we flew a tortuous route to get there. From Geilenkirchen we went to a USAF base at Furstenfelbruck in Southern Germany, thence to Ciampino airport at Rome, where we night-stopped. As the PAI, I flew the dual Vampire on this trip. At Rome we had such a splendid night that amazingly when we took off the following morning my drop tanks failed to feed and so I had to return for another night, while all the rest of the Squadron flew on to Larissa in Greece and thence to Nicosia, the capital of Cyprus. I caught up with them a couple of days later, but the boss was not pleased. We had a good time on detachment and worked and played hard.

Whilst we were in Cyprus, an aircraft at Amman in Jordan urgently needed repairing and the Vampire being our only bird with a spare seat and drop tanks I was authorised to take an NCO engineer and spare parts there. Although it was only a short distance due East, we were not allowed to fly across Israel, so I had to fly South to Fayid, a large RAF base on the Suez Canal, to refuel. We arrived late morning in July, had lunch and took off about 2 pm to go via Aqaba to Amman. The temperature was about 45C, but considerably more a few feet above the black runway. I had not thought to consider there might be any problems but the heavily loaded Vampire struggled down the runway and eventually I realised we might not make it. In fact we became airborne literally just a yard or two before the end of the runway, narrowly missing the runway marker. This was the closest I ever came to writing myself off; I survived by good fortune, nothing else, and that lesson was useful later. We returned to Cyprus the following day, but I made sure we did not attempt take-off in the hottest part of the day.

Our return trip to Germany had to include another leg, because of headwinds; so we first flew from Nicosia to Eskesehir in Turkey, and then retraced our steps from Larissa to Geilenkirchen.

CHAPTER 6

Jim Flemming 1958 (told to me in 1989)

I met Jim Flemming in the late 1960s in the RAAF; subsequently he became an AVM and he told me this tale of being on exchange with USAF:-

"In 1958, being the first TAC squadron to be re-equipped with the F104C Starfighter, the 476th TFS had to do a lot of operational testing of tactics, procedures and capabilities. These included Phase 2 nozzle tests and high altitude operations.

There had been a spate of nozzle failures in the J79 engine fitted to the F104C. It was found that the nozzles, being operated by the engine oil system, were failing to open or close due to sludge on the oil filters, The system was changed so that the nozzles were controlled by the engine fuel system and the problem was solved. The aircraft were being modified at the next major inspection so some squadron aircraft continued to operate with without the oil system control being modified.

For the high altitude tests we were fitted with the early "Moonsuit" pressure suit which was based on the same principle as the "G Suit" but with a full body fitting. Prior to donning the pressure suit you were required to be powdered all over with talcum powder and then don long underwear, inside out, so that the seams would not cause irritation points which could not be reached while wearing the "Moonsuit". Sitting for an hour in the crew room pre-breathing oxygen was a most boring experience. I was scheduled for a high zoom flight to 65,000', and after the required pre-breathing I carried my portable oxygen unit out to my F104C, 56-899, strapped in, converted to the aircraft oxygen system and departed for the high speed area "Stovepipe" up over Death Valley.

My scheduled profile was to climb to 36,000' and level, run out to Mach 1.7 in full AB and a pull to 1.5 G. When the Machmeter showed Mach 2 or better, I was to then increase to 3G for the zoom. At 38,000' the Machmeter was indicating Mach 2.1 with about 35 degrees nose up. The airplane was zooming like an angel and we rapidly passed 50.000' where all indications were normal. As the airplane neared 60,000' I had to throttle back to keep the EGT within limits. The AB blew out and when the throttle was near idle I heard slight "thump" down the back end but all seemed normal. The Starfighter was still climbing but at a reduced angle of attack, about 20 degrees. As 65,000' was reached I stop-cocked the throttle to prevent an over speed over temp and eased the stick forward to about level attitude. The cockpit de-pressurised and I felt the suit pressure come on. It was like being in an all-over G suit and it was difficult to move my arms or legs. The outside light was poor due to the blue/black sky and I had to pull out the instrument panel shades to help the cockpit lighting.

I thought that the aircraft would start to descend but, to my amazement, we kept climbing in a level flight attitude. As we reached 70,000', I eased the stick forward to get a more nose down attitude. The airspeed was about 155 knots and the attitude changed but the Starfighter kept slowly climbing until it peaked at 72,300' when it started to pitch down and descend with wings level. As the speed increased I popped the speed brakes, slowly increased the dive angle, and commenced a glorious high speed dive down to lower levels.

At 40,000' I tried a relight without success. At 35, 000' I tried another relight procedure with same result. At 33,000' I managed to get a relight and was delighted to see the RPM and EGT started to rise. With everything appearing normal I turned towards George passing over the base at 30,000' prior to entering the pattern. At this stage I knew something was wrong, as an increased throttle movement produced the desired RPM but no apparent increase in thrust.

Fortunately, I was aware of the nozzle failure problem where the nozzles remain open and you have a perfectly good engine but no thrust. This was my situation then. The book indicated that level flight could be maintained at 2,000' above sea level in this configuration. With the altitude at George at 1,800' I was not about to test this theory. At 25,000' and descending I declared an emergency and requested a straight-in to Muroc Lake which was almost right in front of me. I turned so that the approach would be to the North East and at 15,000' commenced a high key-low key dead stick approach, which I had practised many times, on to the world's longest runway marked out on the lake bed.

On final approach the engine was developing a little thrust but I continued the dead stick approach, dropping the gear at 250 knots and touching down well into the lake bed at about 185 knots. When I came to a stop, Edwards Tower told me to vacate the airplane and await pick-up. I shut down the engine and when I descended, by hanging over the side of the airplane, I saw that the nozzles were stuck wide open. On looking around I could have been on the Moon; nothing but desert to all horizons. After about fifteen minutes, I was pleased to see a chopper coming over the horizon from the West. The rescue crew took me back to civilization and I had a pleasant time in the Officers Club before being returned to George AFB by car that evening.

After the maintenance crew at the Test Pilot's School had completed the engine oil/fuel nozzle control modification 56-899 flew on for some years before being destroyed in an accident in Spain in the early sixties.

CHAPTER 7

At the end of my tour in Germany I was posted to the staff at the OCU at Chivenor, which now operated Hunters. Hunters were nice to fly except at transonic speeds they were very heavy and impossible to aim; however they gradually improved with succeeding marks over the years. They had an unusual feature, the gun-sight which normally would obstruct the view, was lowered out of sight and only raised when needed by operating a switch. The sharp metal was covered by a thick rubber pad just in front of your face and was known to us as "the humane killer".

I took over a Flight from an American Exchange Captain (later 3-star General) who at his dining out joined us in over-indulging in the free sherry before dinner. The CO made flattering remarks on this occasion, talked about how he had advanced understanding between our nations, and thanked him for his service. At which in reply he made the shortest speech I have ever heard:- "Sir, and fellow members, there are three things for which we have yet to find any use – the tits on a man, the balls on the Pope and a vote of thanks from the staff" at which he sat down, or collapsed!

The second course I had charge of was to convert onto Hunters No 6 Squadron, Royal Iraqi Air Force. After two speared in, and I think four quit "because it is too dangerous", the rest were confined to flying when there was no cloud at all to be seen. The CO of the Squadron was the only one who might have actually passed our course – and not only because he happily drank whisky in the bar.

The best thing that happened to me on that tour was attendance at DFLS "Day Fighter Leaders School" at Central Fighter Establishment West Raynham. All flying completed regardless of weather (the preceding course had lost 5 aircraft on one sortie) and truly hairy. For example on one eight v eight dog fight I was pursuing a pair of Hunters in a maximum turn at very low level when suddenly there was a plan view of two more Hunters missing me literally by a few feet. "Gee that was close" I thought, then realised that if we continued as before our circles would intercept again very soon. No sooner thought than it happened, missed again by a few feet. On this course all flying was done to the limits and I don't think anyone ever got back to Raynham with enough fuel to go round again on an overshoot.

Marvellous, wonderful course! However it was on this course that I started to suffer from a strange vertigo, which only affected me when I was at extreme altitude. I am frightened of heights normally, for example I hated going up the Eiffel Tower. Flying at height had never been a problem before: now, flying at 25,000 -30,000 feet was comfy, but going up to 45,000 feet I became scared of the drop! Ridiculous, but true; naturally I could not tell anyone, because I probably would have been taken off flying.

After my Chivenor tour I was sent to the best ground job I could have – to the famous Bentley Priory, HQ Fighter Command, posting fighter pilots. It was plainly necessary for me to visit all the day fighter Squadrons regularly (there were 20 of them then) and to this end there was a communications flight at Bovingdon, nearby. On the flight were two Meteors, one a Mark 8 and the other a Night/All weather Mk14. I think I was the only chap who flew them – whenever I telephoned to book one it was always available. In addition to squadron visits I had also to do "P staff" pre-AOC's inspections at all the bases, so I got quite a bit of flying. Also, whenever there was an exercise on I was allowed to join a Squadron temporarily. Knowing that I was going to select their next posting, people were pretty nice to me.

It was at Fighter Command that I met and admired a senior officer I shall call Chris. Sixteen years previously he had been commanding a fighter Squadron, shortly after Battle of Britain; the pressure having eased somewhat, they were stood down for a weekend and took advantage of the respite by having a Ball in the Mess. A glamorous creature, Chris had imported an equally glamorous girl from London for the Ball, which he and she left a little early. Nearby was a pretty tidy hotel, where they were established.

They were woken at about 4 am by a telephone and a voice said "I'm sorry to disturb you Sir, but I understand that you are staying here with a lady who is not your wife." (In those days people were much more moral than today.) "This is a respectable hotel Sir with a high reputation; I do not wish to offend my other guests and so I must ask you to leave straight away. There will be no charge for your accommodation, but I must ask you to leave NOW".

Somewhat horrified Chris woke the blonde and told her they were leaving, got dressed and crept along in darkness to the stairs. Descending gingerly in the dark, they were about 6 steps from the bottom when all the lights went on to show all the squadron's pilots gathered in the foyer clapping and laughing.

Nowadays the RAF aerobatic team is called the Red Arrows and flies trainer aircraft painted red. Before them there was the Black Arrows, flying black-painted Hunters of 111 Squadron. This was plainly the best formation aerobatic team in the world. They had decided to perform a 22 aircraft close formation loop, which when it took place at the Farnborough air show prompted the Chief of USAF to say to our chief, Dermot Boyle "Marshal – you win!" One of my tasks was to provide 111 with suitable pilots, so I had to spend quite a lot of time with them; formation aero pilots are normally "left hand men" or "right hand men", depending on which side they prefer to fly. They spent a lot of time waiting in crew-rooms, normally playing Bridge. One day I was told "We need a left hand man who plays ACOL"! Yes - I got them one.

Happily "my" Meteor 14 was ideal for air to air photography; it had a seat in the back for the photographer and a clear canopy, with no obstructions. So we took out its radar and the guns, thereby greatly improving its performance, and I was the natural candidate to tag on the outside of various formations to obtain photos. In my two seasons with treble one I flew many photographers taking superb pictures (and of some other aero teams). I have several examples from Mike Chase, a well-known and brilliant photographer, a huge strong ex-commando who was in the Royal Air Force public relations branch. He had to hold his heavy camera (with plates) up high and take immaculate pictures even while I was pulling over 3 "G". Altogether an excellent "ground" tour!

CHAPTER 8

Graham Neil

Graham is a good friend from RAAF days, he was a FAC in Vietnam and eventually rose to 2 star rank. His story goes:- "In about 1961-62, I can't be more specific because my logbooks are in storage, when Butterworth was home to 78 Fighter Wing, the two Sabre Squadrons thrived upon the rivalry and one-upmanship which was the order of the day. In those days, it was usual for RAAF personnel and their families to return to Australia by sea and it had become the practice amongst squadrons to stage ad hoc flypasts over the passenger liners as a farewell gesture to the returnees. It goes without saying that some of the flypasts exhibited some spectacular flying out to sea. But past performances of daring were soon to become eclipsed by sheer accident. Having ascertained the P and 0 ship's sailing time, and having calculated the time she would take to reach a position off the northern part of Penang Island, each mission on our squadron programme was examined and a flight, in which I was No 4, was chosen to do the flypast. The prime aim of the exercise was to execute 2 v 2 ACT; a higher joker fuel was set so as to allow time for a flypast to be tacked onto the end of the sortie. At the briefing we were told that, because we could not be too sure of the ship's position near the end of our sortie, we would have to play the flypast very much by ear. As a safety measure 1 and 2 were to keep the ship on their left, and 3 and 4 on their right during any flypast, which was to be in close pairs formation.

The mission proceeded normally until 'joker' was called by No 2. The flight headed back towards Penang and the ship was soon sighted in an ideal position just to the north of the island. 1 and 2 dived towards the ship and 3 and 4, further out in battle formation were unfortunately caught napping and dropped back into long trail by about three miles. We plunged down from 20,000 ft to ensure that we passed the ship with at least 600 kts.

Unfortunately, we had dropped back too far in trail and by the time we were well established in the dive when No 1, having completed his first pass, called that we would do 'one more pass - same rules'. Having seen 1 and 2 fly past the ship and hold down before executing a high wing-over back towards the ship, both 3 and 4 assumed that 1 and 2 would do their second pass on a reciprocal heading back towards base - smart thinking, since we were not exactly flush for fuel. We did our first pass knowing the position of 1 and 2. We then executed a wing-over in the same piece of sky in which we had earlier seen 1 and 2 do the same. On our second pass at about mast-head level, No 3 called that he was pulling up - no other explanation was offered. I assumed he had had a bird-strike or perhaps a HYD 1 problem, but being a steely-eyed wing-man I pressed on to complete our part of the flypast. I did not even consider following No 3 when he pulled up, after all - wasn't the main thing to complete the job that had to be done? I had 610 kts down near B-deck level, nicely trimmed out (a JC problem was not unknown in the Sabre), when a small dot on the horizon turned out to be a smoking dot - turned out to be No 1. I couldn't obey international rules and turn right (into the ship); I didn't want to pull up, perhaps into No 1, and I couldn't go left in case No 1 chose to break right. So I went down as low as I dared; we smoked past each other, self low, at a closing speed of at least 1200 kts. It transpired that No 1 was at about A-deck level and I was at about F-deck level (if the ship had six decks). We passed each other with apparently perfect timing – exactly amidships.

We carried out a shaky recovery and debrief during which I learnt that No 3 had sighted 1 and 2 doing their second pass in the same direction as their first pass - whereas we were flying ours on a reciprocal heading!

Later congratulatory letters sent by RAAF members, even from bomber crews, congratulating the Squadron on our flamboyant display and exceptional sense of timing were insufficient compensation for the shock that complacency and over-confidence had led to.

The lesson couldn't have been too salutary though because, some years later, after having completed my QFI course and having experienced about one year on flying instruction, I found myself in the unusual situation of sharing the circuit at Point Cook with only one other Winjeel. Usually the circuit was cluttered with about 10 to 14 Winjeels - perhaps the fact that it was the lunch hour had something to do with it. I was to have my student practise glide circuits using a 1500 ft circuit and the other aircraft was carrying out flapless circuits using a 1000 ft circuit. On down-wind the other aircraft was seen ahead and below, both students called 'base glide' and 'base flapless' respectively. I soon lost sight of the other aircraft but didn't concern myself too much about it because the other Winjeel on its flapless approach could be expected to use Lane 4 on the outside, and, besides, he was dual. On finals I kept a beady eye out to starboard to look out for the other Winjeel but on each check saw nothing. I therefore assumed that the other aircraft was hidden behind our starboard wing. On late, late, final at about 50 ft the realization came to me that any aircraft under our wing would have to be so close to us, because of the proximity of the ground, that its relative size would have it showing most parts of its fuselage ahead and behind our own wing. I quickly took over from Bloggs and as I increased power in the overshoot I saw the silver and day-glo orange blur of the other aircraft underneath us. As I harshly pulled back on the control column I expected that our tail plane would have to strike the other aircraft on rotation (we were that close) but we managed to fly out without even touching each other. The other aircraft ran to a jagged halt and the QFI called it a day - our main wheels had gone astride his canopy. Both students had been immaculately lined up on the centre of Lane 1 which was reserved for glide circuits. The other QFI knew he was in the wrong lane but assumed we would see them. Nothing had been heard from tower or the Duty Instructor in the 'pie-cart' because they had each over-transmitted their warnings simultaneously.

We too called it a day and made our next landing a full-stop. After near-normal debriefs, mutual QFI debriefs and talks with the Flight Commander and the Chief Flying Instructor, the C0 was briefed on the incident. He was a flamboyant type not without some hectic wartime fighter experience and personal test pilot experience at being on the losing end of quite a few aircraft crashes. His closing words reminded me of the lesson which should have stuck with me for life after the Sabre flypast incident - "Don't assume nothing".

CHAPTER 9

In 1960 I left the fighter world and was assigned to Photo Recce Canberras. I was sent as a Flight Commander to 13 Squadron in Cyprus. Our area of responsibility was enormous – North to Russian border, South to Lesotho, and East to Iran. We did virtually no training, all our sorties were operational – i.e. in support of our intelligence services or mapping. We had more or less permanent detachments in North Africa, Bahrain, Aden and Nairobi. We operated PR7 Canberras, which had a huge extra fuel tank taking up what would have been half the bomb-bay. The squadron was expert at long-range flying and I can still remember the technique – fly at best airframe drag speed and best engine economy, cruise climbing as a result. A PR7 once flew from Wytton in UK to Aden, nonstop!

A favourite detachment was Nairobi; there was one problem; going to and from Nairobi one had to pass the ITF (Inter Tropical Front) – a band of extremely vicious thunderstorms. Dangerous to go under (we couldn't afford the fuel anyway to go down to low level) and too high to go over. We were not equipped with weather radar so we just had to look and guess which was the best way through. One of the other Squadrons lost a Canberra in one – it was ripped to pieces. Made for some scary times.

Before Nairobi airport was built we operated out of RAF Eastleigh. This was not really suitable for jet aircraft, as the tarmac was extremely short (from memory about 100 yards) and after that you were on murram – which was pure dust when dry and thick mud when wet. We had "rules" about aborting take-off if you had not reached a speed of 85 knots by the end of the tarmac and landing had to be very careful. A road crossing the approach had traffic lights on it but these were frequently ignored, causing extra palpitations when performing a hazardous short landing and simultaneously trying to miss a cyclist.

One of our aircraft had had a major unserviceability there and after several months it had been repaired and was ready for collection. My navigator and I went to collect it. This involved travelling down to Nairobi by civil air, which necessitated a night stop in Beirut and another in Cairo! Eventually we got to Nairobi, somewhat hung over.

There had been no air test done and the murram was wet so I did not want to attempt a take-off with full fuel for the long trip back to Cyprus with a possibly dodgy aircraft. So I decided to do an air test at the same time as a short trip to Entebbe, in Uganda, just the other side of Lake Victoria. Never been there before, but we had no problems. Having filled up with fuel we set forth. A couple of hours later I said to Pete Ross, my navigator "We're not going to make it – think of a diversion". Without missing a beat he replied "turn right – Khartoum – what's the matter?" We had in fact got an oxygen leak and it would not have lasted the whole trip, yet it was necessary to fly at height to obtain the range required. So we diverted to Khartoum for oxygen – first time we had been there too. It was blisteringly hot, but remembering my experience at Fayid we dug out all the manuals and discovered the runway was definitely too short for take-off until the temperature dropped. (We were very confidently treated by Ali the ground mechanic who looked after visitors, so later we went there quite often.) Eventually when it cooled down a bit we got away, using every inch of the runway. The book was right.

On another occasion we were urgently required in Bahrain. Flying over Syria or Israel was not allowed, so we had to go round them to the north. We took off from Cyprus in the evening and my navigator had a "fix" i.e. a definite position as dusk was falling and we crossed the Turkish coast. Soon afterwards he reported that not only his Doppler navigation aid had stopped working, but so had everything else he had except his compass. So we proceeded on "dead reckoning" i.e. working out our position by how fast we were going in what direction and allowing for forecasted winds. We had both been to Bahrain many times before and would use their radar when we got there.

The visibility closed down and eventually, not having had a fix for over three hours, the nav said he reckoned we were close. I called Bahrain approach to be told that there was a severe dust storm which had not only put out their radar but even their direction finding equipment. Our flying instruments were OK as was our radio altimeter, but there was nothing to see out in the dust storm. We did not really have enough fuel to divert (there were only a few desert strips around anyway, since neither Kuwait nor Dubai airports had been built yet), so I told the nav to get us right overhead according to his sums and descended to about 1200 feet. I started a square search pattern, which has ever increasing legs, on instruments, with the nav lying prone in the nose looking out. Still could see nothing. On about the 7th leg of the pattern he saw a light, which on inspection turned out to be Bahrain airfield. He had done really well. We told the tower we had them in sight and called for landing clearance – granted. The visibility was so bad I now had to set up a timed circuit, also on instruments. Thank God for stop watches! Made a reasonable approach through the dust and landed safely. After we were down the Tower asked "What is your position?" – they could not see us, even though we had lights on and were only about 60 yards away.

Our detachments to Aden (Khormaksar) were interesting. Among other activities there was sporadic fighting in the Radfan, an area north of Aden. The tribesmen would frequently attack our troops and then report to the Foreign Office representatives who would replace their empty cartridges with live ones! Occasionally the RAF would strafe and bomb a village as punishment and we would afterwards complete a low level post-strike recce. This was not surprisingly resented by the villagers, who would fire their rifles and even throw things at us.

On another occasion our photos of an unfriendly country showed Surface to Air missiles being rotated to point at us as we went by. Later I discovered that the missile operators had been calling their masters for permission to shoot at us; luckily no reply came in time.

Soon afterwards the Squadron re-equipped with PR9 Canberras. The RAF had wanted a high altitude PR capability but was denied a new aircraft, but could have a modified version of an existing one. So they cheated. The result was this strange aircraft which looked at first blush like a Canberra, but had virtually nothing in common with it. The originals were made by English Electric, the PR9s by Shorts of Belfast, known to us as "Irish Elastic". The wing area was about double, the engines nearly twice the power, hydraulic controls, alligator-opening bubble canopy and the nav sat on an ejector seat in the hinged nose. No parts in common either, even things like fuel cocks were not the same. There were only two squadrons of them, us in Cyprus and 39 in Malta and with all the spares in Ireland we had to wait a while whenever we needed something. Eventually at my suggestion they shipped all the spares, by boat, to the Mediterranean. Unfortunately the boat sank in the Bay of Biscay!

We aircrew of PR9s were treated as special, in common with Lightning pilots. We had to go on a special aviation medicine course where we were fitted with goldfish-bowl helmets (very expensive and which I never wore again) and experienced an explosive decompression to 60,000 feet. We also had special uniforms issued free and given extra rations.

The PR9 was a pleasure to fly. It had an auto-pilot for those long transit legs and so powerful were the engines that one could take off with much less than full power. No longer was a combination of hot weather and short runway a problem. Its ceiling was where the limiting Mach and the stalling speed coincided. Very little of the flying was at extreme altitude so I did not often have to control my funny vertigo. By this time I was OK up to about 45,000 ft, but above about 55,000 I would lower my seat so I felt more secure and less likely to fall out! I also had a nearly irresistible urge to lower the undercarriage. Mad.

My tour came to an end, I was promoted and to my amazement I became the Squadron Commander. The easiest take-over ever – I knew the people, the aircraft and the work, so I embarked on another tour with great happiness.

Approaching Khormaksar (Aden) one hot afternoon, I called for landing clearance and made an approach which turned out to be a bad one, too fast and so I called "overshooting" and went round again. My next attempt was much better, but as I touched down I was still not really quite right and so I called "rolling" and took off again without stopping. On my third attempt I called for landing clearance and the cheeky tower operator replied "You are clear to land, roll or overshoot as you wish". This story got told a fair bit too often back at the Squadron, but I hope it in fact helped the junior pilots; many major accidents have been caused by pilots not admitting mistakes.

Nairobi's new airport was now available for us and arriving late one evening somewhat tired from Cyprus, we found some turbulence and extremely heavy rain reducing visibility to virtually zero. The Airport had ILS (Instrument Landing System) and we had a semi automatic ILS in the PR9. (The power settings were manual, but the auto pilot would follow the glide path). I had checked Nairobi's system before and was confident in it: the GCA (Ground Control Approach) could not see us through the rain, so I elected to do an ILS. I was tired and reckoned the auto was at least as good as, and probably better than, me so I made the complete approach on auto pilot and only took it out just as we touched down. Not quite within regulations and bad airmanship – but it was called a "Landing" system, wasn't it?

One other trip is worth mentioning. During the Cypriot civil war in January 1964 our intelligence people were trying to keep track of a particular person. It was believed he had driven his car up into the mountains and was staying in a particular village for the night. I was asked if we could photograph the village; this involved night photography.

Night photo then required flashes to be dropped sequentially, from a precise height above the terrain to be photographed – in this instance 1200 feet, if I remember correctly. Having discussed it with my Nav Leader, Jock Hay, we decided to go. On a dark overcast night we had to fly well below the alarmingly close hills around us as we went up the valley. The trouble from my point of view was I had to lower the seat fully, to go as low as possible in the cockpit and fly on instruments until the task was done (I had to trust the navigator completely; if I had looked out I would have been blinded by the flashes) and then the valley ended and we had to climb steeply out. It was not practical to descend straight to the target, so we had to go up the valley. Our flashes went off at about one second intervals with big bangs (and of course a very bright light, illuminating the ground). Then I had to use all the PR9's great power to climb steeply out of the valley to miss the hills. We completed two runs at the target, using about 25 flashes on each. The following day we had reports of two aircraft firing rockets at each other! I believe this to be the only actual operational low-level night photo operation ever tasked by the RAF. I wrote up the sortie to get Jock Hay a well-deserved Air Force Cross.

After a posting to the Ministry of Defence (not much enjoyed) I left the RAF and joined the RAAF in 1967 for a 4 year short service tour. I offered myself as a photo-reconnaissance expert, but they thought they were hiring a very well qualified fighter pilot, so we were both disappointed. I was posted to become a flight commander on a Mirage Squadron. Yet I had been away from fighters for 10 years, was getting older, and now there was a totally new generation of aircraft. Adding to my difficulties, I had trouble understanding the Australian accent and idiom, especially on the radio; flying was done with American procedures, with which I was completely unfamiliar (terms like "Base" and "Initial" were foreign to me, I was accustomed to the RAF's "Downwind" and "Finals"). Finally there was considerable resentment, by some, of an interloping Pommy being posted to one of the most highly prized appointments in the RAAF, though most people were friendly, understanding and supportive. It quickly became apparent, even before I joined the squadron, that I was out of my depth. I frankly wasn't up to it. So my posting was changed to Operations Officer at the fighter base at Williamtown and in my four year ground tour there I managed to get about 650 hours, nearly all in the Australian Sabre. After a year or two I managed to get myself back into the ways of fighter pilots and I wangled a place on a Mirage Conversion course where I got about 15 hrs solo including a high speed run at night, exceeding Mach2. The rest of my RAAF time was uneventful, except I made some very good friends, some of whom you've heard from here; another was

CHAPTER 10

Pete Larard,

who was awarded the DSO in Vietnam. So I asked him for his war stories, and here they are:- Contribution by Peter Larard, Wing Commander, RAAF Retired. Sidewinder 31, then Jade 01.

A war story is specified. Well OK! More than half a lifetime ago, indeed probably in a different life altogether nearly 50 years ago, like 35 other RAAF fighter pilots I got involved in the war in Vietnam in 1968-69 seconded to the US 7th Air Force to fly US aircraft as an airborne Forward Air Controller. You may have heard and understand the term! My 12 months of operations was split between support of the 1st US Infantry Division (Third Brigade) and about the four to five final months with the 1st Australian Task Force, both in 111 Corps area, hence the two callsigns. I remember my time with the USAF and US Army with both joy and pride, but detail of what actually took place during individual sorties is not so readily available.

But back to the war story. In fairy tale land it could start with, "There I was at 1500 feet over tropical jungle, sweating like a running tap in the Bronco's huge greenhouse cockpit, continually rolling the machine around to avoid the mostly light automatic weapons ground fire, smoothly and effectively manipulating switches and volume controls on at least four of the bird's five two-way radios, keeping me and fighters clear of artillery fire while giving support to the grunts in close contact with enemy below, first by precisely identifying them, and then marking the aiming points for the fighter pilots with white phosphorus rockets, then controlling the fighters delivering their napalm and stuff sometimes as close as 20 metres from the nearest friendlies, vital continuous liaison with all agencies persisting. Pretty soon the bad guys would flee leaving a body-count of KBA (Killed By Air) which I would pass to the fighter lead as I cleared his flight on their return to base. Down below the young lieutenant platoon commander and most of his boys would be still there to tell their Moms of their part in the war."

That's in the ideal world. It often did not work out as perfectly, but essentially in our part of 111 Corps area that's what it was about, working in close support of troops in contact. Of course there were slips. It never did to be in a hurry although reaction timing was often critical. There was always a certain urgency; for some reason guys getting shot at speak quicker, louder, and in a bit higher octave. It took a while for some US speak to become recognizable to my Aussie lexicon. and vice versa I am sure. Napalm often dudded. It always paid to follow the fighter in his dive towards the target prepared to light up a non burning can with a WP rocket. Ordnance delivery errors were just not acceptable for close in work. FACs got to know which squadrons were the best at it and would use only those guys for the really close work, nevertheless, always starting a bit further out in case the fighter pilot was "off his game" on that day.

Come on! The war story! OK there must have been one or two in just over 400 trips in both the OV-10 and the O-2 including over 100 on TIC missions. In general, like all of us, I got shot at. I became most vindictive about that and shot back with as much help as I could get. I think we seriously won all the Troops-In-Contact encounters of the type I recall. In fact I often remark that if that was a war that we lost I wonder what we did to our enemies in those which we won! Luckily perhaps, certainly thankfully, I made it through without being involved in a short round (where friendlies take damage), and none of our TACP FACs were lost during my time. I regard being able to talk about one's involvement in a war 40 years after the event as pretty happy situation. Here's some of how it went.

The FAC U! Phan Rang RVN, November 1968. At last! Before that was the BUIS in Saigon, God knows what the initials meant, but it was home for a number of Australian and US military officers. I have no idea what they were doing, but it was a lodging place on quite a big scale. Included was a bar and a dining hall with really quite good meals, very American, in the offing. My room neighbour was Sqn Ldr David Oxenham DFC, shot down in a Wellington over Europe somewhere in the early 1940s, and our ex actual neighbour at Jalan Bungah Melati in Penang, late 1964. David was about to return to Australia in late '68 and was working at COMRAAFV where A/Cmdre Fred Robey had just taken over. My secondment to the US 7th Airforce was initially to the TACC, Tactical Air Control Centre located at Ton Son Nhut, the main airport for Saigon. The TACC controlled all offensive air activity in both North and South Vietnam.

In 1968 Saigon was a bugger of a place to be!

One rode about in an open bus which picked up officers from the BUIS and delivered them to their various places of duty around Saigon. I had to get what seemed like about 15 ks to Ton Son Nhut airport. En route, while stopping at traffic lights, if they were working, and whatever, the bus was ever subject to the attention of ratbag kids of the city possibly armed by the VC and urged to kill Americans! They couldn't identify Americans from Australians, as if that mattered. There was a well defined risk of kids lobbing a hand grenade into the back of the vehicle! This was not my scene! But not only that, at the TACC I was assigned to the FRAG shop which produced the daily mission orders for the both the USAF and the USN air strike forces in both North and South Vietnam. The TACC was headed up by a one star general, a Brigadier General with whom I had spent quite a bit of time initially. He and the rest of his officers never understood that a Wing Commander, as I was, was a rank, equivalent of lieutenant colonel. In the USAF a wing commander was a respected senior position. They commanded large wings and were senior full colonels. Every USAF officer would stand up and salute me as I entered a room or passed them in the corridor or on a street. They did not need hats on to do this. USAF enlisted men on the other hand just stared but rarely saluted! Fragmentary Orders or Frags described targets, weapons loads, times on target, mission strength, and the unit allocated the task. Often the orders went further even specifying tactics such as attack directions. By about day two at this it was obvious that very little real priority was being given to tactics. We "fragged" missions against one bridge in North Vietnam at the same time on target for four or five consecutive days, and because it was close to the DMZ specifying the same attack direction. I could not believe it and complained like hell! I was told that to change the tape which controlled the machinery sending the orders, using the existing secure communications signals system, was too time consuming. I had always volunteered for this duty in Vietnam to fly, not to risk a grenade under my bus seat on the way to work so that I could contribute to sending fighter pilots on poorly conceived missions. I fronted the General and explained to him that I had "got enough" from the Frag Shop and asked to be transferred to forward air controller (FAC) duties. He agreed and I was assigned to the in-country FAC training facility, locally known as the FAC U at Phan Rang, to check out on the new OV-10A Bronco with the view to becoming an Air Liaison Officer (ALO) at a US Army unit.

Flying the OV-10 was always going to be enjoyable. It was a business-like very capable looking piece of kit. 41 foot wingspan, twin Allison turbo props giving 1500hp together, full STOL capability, five weapons attachment points on sponsons and in-built 4x 30 cal Brownings, a cargo hold which could carry five equipped paratroopers, very good all around and down visibility from the tandem cockpits, more radios than a brace of command posts, and rocket extraction escape seats good if wings level at zero altitude and 2000ft/max rate of descent. Negative G was not permitted, otherwise it was fully aerobatic, and performance was similar to a WW2 piston fighter. I found it a great weapons platform although in my time we were not permitted to arm the guns nor carry high explosive stores on the sponsons. We were limited to Willy Petes, white phosphorous rockets for target marking. Funny thing, some of them seemed to explode on impact! The airforce never used the cargo hold for troops either, but it came in very handy for transporting many cases of Vic Bitter and other comforts of home up-country from Vung Tau. The only down side to that sweet little aircraft was its lack of air conditioning. Low altitude tropical operations in that big green-house cockpit could become pretty uncomfortable. As another somewhat quirky feature, you mounted it from the right hand side. No one would try to get on a horse or into a fighter from the right!

The OV-10 came into the US inventories first as a Navy and Marines asset. Flying it was taught according to naval techniques. This meant crashing the machine onto the runway in a hanging on power semi stalled situation, as one would if landing on a deck. The undercarriage was massive and clearly up to taking that sort of punishment, but I was not built for that sort of thing. It handled beautifully if greased onto the ground using full aerodynamic braking. Reverse pitch from the props was available, and if executed correctly, you could stop it inside the distance previously used, having by contrast caused very little if any brake and tyre wear. 57% of the lift from its wings came from propeller slipstream so that an engine failure below a safe single-engine climb away speed could be quite critical. Aircraft and crew were lost because people did not understand that limitation. When eventually arming the Bronco in FAC operations was permitted I am sure local air power became more effective. We would often expend WPs in frustrated attempts to engage enemy forces. Maybe we burned some of them!

RAAF No 2 squadron flying the old Canberra level bombers was also based at Phan Rang. I had several pals there including the CO, J A Whitehead. He put me up while I was at the FAC U for about 2 weeks in his luxurious US supplied air conditioned 2 bedroomed trailer with ensuites. I could have got used to that!

Lai Khe was an old rubber plantation about 35 nautical miles direct north of Saigon near the Song Be River. In 1969 it was home to the Third Brigade, and the HQ of the US First Infantry Division, the Big Red One, as their shoulder patch showed. As they said, "If yr gotta be one yr might as well be a big red one". I was assigned as ALO to the 3rd Brigade in charge of a USAF TACP (Tactical Air Control Party) comprising between 5 and 6 OV-10s, as many FACs, radio specialists, crew chiefs for maintenance support, and a few vehicles (Jeeps and support equipment). We lived in a basic "hootch" or hut provided by the army which by self help had been made reasonably comfortable. Our enlisted men were in similar about 50 metres away. Beds were separated by steel locker cum wardrobes which showed numerous hits by bits of shrapnel from incoming VC and NVA 122mm rockets. Toiletries were performed using a multi holer long drop latrine a hundred yards away, and a cold shower using water from a salvaged aircraft drop tank mounted on top of a conex. It was sometimes made hot with a petrol-burning immersion heater. There was a refrigerator, a telephone to the Brigade Tactical Ops Centre, a bar counter, and a small stove for cooking. The "living room" of the hootch was decorated with the spoils of war. On the wall were mounted a couple of captured AK 47s, a flag or two and other "souvenirs" of the day. Alongside was a substantial bunker with six or eight bunks into which we fled during incoming rocket or mortar fire. We could eat at the nearby chow hall, Army food cafeteria style with not a lot to recommend it, or we could cook our own using our meagre facilities but with ingredients traded from all kinds of sources. The US logistic system in the whole of South Vietnam, I am convinced, depended upon local trading. Trading included Jeeps etc. We traded to get a weapons carrying vehicle (A Kawasaki Mule I think) at Lai Khe to enable us to load rockets on our aircraft. The USAF support system would not provide. We had to trade with an army heavy lift chopper crew who had in the dead of night illegally airlifted this vehicle from the huge stores base at Long Bin. OK it was stealing by the letter of the law, but the equipment so stolen got to be used genuinely as part of the war effort. As examples, the Australian combat boots were leather and superior to the standard US issue. A pair of the Aussie boots (bought from the store at Vung Tau) was worth a case (56 lbs) of frozen steak from the US Army cook house! Hard liquor (whisky etc) was not available to US enlisted men. A bottle or two of "tradin' whusky" might bring forth a case of frozen Aussie lobster tails. There was actually one time when another Aussie FAC at Lai Khe came in from a mission asking "what are we eating tonight?" and when told said "not bloody lobster again!" We also dined by invitation with the brigade commander in his mess. That was more proper and much more popular!

There was one night in the brigade commander's dining room when Flt Lt Doug Riding decided to teach the delicate effect of an "after burner", or "flaming hooker" as our USAF mates called it, to our brigade CO, Colonel Bob Haldane. Hindsight tells me that Bob Haldane well knew the whole story of a burning glass of drambuie from his WW2 experience in Britain in the US Army Air Corps, but nevertheless, he fearlessly played the game. The "game" was of course to start and finish a burning glass of drambuie leaving it empty but still burning. I was with him in the C in C chopper the next morning when he had to put up with comment and glances at the Fu Man Chu moustache style of the very red burn marks flowing down either side of his mouth, accentuated by Bob's Nordic blonde complexion.

Another morning in the CinC chopper with Bob Haldane was a bit more exciting. This is a story I regret having to chronicle when I do not remember the name of the young US Army captain flying the Huey that morning, to whose airmanship and skill we all owe our survival. The scene was an NVA bunker entrance which we had discovered about a klick or two from a fire support base. Artillery was ordered up and to keep the bad fellows' heads down while it was coming we decided to engage with the CinC chopper. Fire power at our disposal comprised the two door 30 cal gunners, I had my Colt AR 15, and an M79 40 mm grenade launcher with a full box of ammo, which the Colonel always kept for such an emergency. The grenade launcher was obviously the best bet. I had the window seat so he had to lean across me trying to lob one into the opening, one round per pass! On every second pass (from the same direction) Bob Haldane handed me the weapon to try my luck. By about the sixth pass I said, "hey, come on, stop this, sooner or later these guys are going to get pissed off with us, and realizing that we apparently could not hit a bull in the arse from a yard away, they are going to come out and stitch us up". OK I was wrong until about the fourteenth pass when we still had not put a grenade into the opening. They stepped out with a few AKs and gave it back to us. The chopper took I don't know how many hits, hydraulic oil was everywhere but miraculously nobody was hit and the bird was still flying. By the skill of the pilot we made it into the fire support base nearby without further casualty, but a Hook (heavy lift chopper) was needed to get that Huey out. No problem, the Commander got a new one the next day!

The long drop toilet facility back at Lai Khe could be hazardous. Every morning a group of Vietnamese women labourers would burn the spoil using diesel or something similar. If you were using the dunny at the time this was not all that comfortable. Just knowing they were there was sort of constipating in itself. Ken Mitchell and I were able to get hold of a proper toilet and cistern from the RAAF at Vung Tau. We co-opted a tame VC to hand dig a huge hole to fit an old damaged boiler to function as a septic tank. We connected the loo to it with a 5 inch flexible fuel pipe. Another conex mounted drop tank supplied the water. We begged cement and sand etc from the local works people to make a concrete floor and lo! An ensuite! We had the only flushing and undercover toilet at Lai Khe outside the Division commander's and the Brigade commander's quarters. We became very popular.

In the first half of 1969 Lai Khe took sporadic frequent incoming fire from 122m rockets and mortars, not a lot of rounds, mostly at night, and seemingly randomly aimed. The division base was enclosed in a rather large perimeter protected by seismic sensors, visual and radar anti personnel surveillance, and patrols equipped with what became known as the "squirrel gun", a jeep-mounted 5 inch swivelling rocket projectile launcher firing antipersonnel rounds, This weapon produced a heartening whoosh-boom sound, making one pleased it was a friendly. Permanently located there were 8 inch and 155mm artillery units which took target information from mortar detecting radar, and which within minutes fired counter rocket/counter mortar retaliatory fire for what seemed like about 40 minutes after we received the 5 or 10 rounds of incoming. The noise was horrendous. Our OV-10s were revetted and escaped significant damage but several unrevetted army choppers were lost in my time there, and the division suffered casualties and fatalities from random hits on sleeping quarters. Had the NVA/ VC been able to better target their ordnance against living quarters I believe the almost nightly attacks would have been much more effective. As it was they were primarily of scare value. We took to sleeping in our bunker which had six or eight two tier bunks along a narrow walkway. Crowded bunkers amount to a very personal experience requiring special and specified behaviour. Breaking wind was gazetted as a hanging offence. We enjoyed the relative immunity from the rockets until one morning when we discovered one very large fresh snake skin on the ground alongside the bunks, a large King Cobra had sloughed in there with us over night. The new bunker commander was immediately accredited and most FACs decided the incoming in their regular beds was a less risky option. Gene Harrison, an ALO after me at Lai Khe, in his book,

"A Lonely Kind of War", reports this incident as occurring in his time. He treated that fact more than somewhat loosely.

The beds had essential mosquito nets. Initially I slept with mine tucked in under the mattress all round. No malaria risk for me! Then the night came when I first experienced this incoming fire. As I had been advised, there is absolutely no doubt about whether fire is incoming or not. So, up and to the bunker asap. Only I could not find my way out of the wretched mosquito net. I am still being reminded, 40 years later, by the other Australian there at the time, Ken Mitchell, of my comments and antics as I continued with successive but abortive attempts to free myself from that net (he always exaggerates the detail).

The 3rd Brigade's area of operations (AO) extended broadly from the Iron Triangle in the south, up Thunder Road to the east to just north of a line across from the Michelin Rubber plantation then generally south down the Song Be River back to the Iron Triangle. We sometimes operated special missions outside that, such as taking part in new weapons experimentation with new cluster bomb units (CBUs), we controlled defoliation missions and others such as Ark Lights (B-52 strikes), but nearly all our work was confined to our AO. We routinely flew visual recce missions to cover the daylight hours. This gave us an airborne alert in the form of a FAC airborne in the area in daylight hours. The VR missions were used to control the day's pre-planned air strikes as well as any troops in contact (TIC) or emergency situation which may arise. We flew night operations when night troop insertions involved preparatory and/or supportive air strikes and we scrambled to control offensive air support when enemy night ground attacks took place. FACs got to know the detail of the area minutely like the paddocks on one's own farm. Any fresh movement evidence was immediately apparent to our eyes. The presence of the FAC aircraft buzzing around the AO in itself became a comfort to the local ground commanders. As FACs do we provided communications assistance, sometimes precise navigation help, local impending weather information, guidance for medivac (dustoff) operations, and we were on hand to adjust artillery if required. Long Range Recon Patrols whose positions had been compromised frequently used our support to enable their safe emergency extraction. A FAC nearly always flew as part of the battle staff of the Brigade Commander in his CinC chopper. At Lai Khe it was a busy but always interesting, sometimes quite challenging, and I believe very successful operation.

Perhaps the most outstanding success of my TACP in my time at Lai Khe took place on a night which I personally had spent on some admin task involving an overnight at Vung Tau. This was the defence against a major ground attack on Fire Support Base Oran. The 2nd/28th Battalion, Black Lions, came very close to being over-run. Flight Lieutenant Ken Mitchell, RAAF, was one of the FAC stars of that night. The enemy was stopped literally on the wire by effective use of close air support, leaving a large number of their attacking force behind as they withdrew. But there were many other examples of highly successful air-supported operations against NVA and Viet Cong. The 2nd/28th fellows were forever calling to our hootch to see if there was anything we needed! Some great nights of debriefing followed! Rescues of LRRPs (long Range Reconnaissance Patrols) elements figured large. These small groups, sometimes comprised of only a half dozen or so soldiers, seemed frequently to find their positions compromised and themselves under attack from sizeable enemy forces. Their only survival options lay in prompt chopper extraction. Too often these extractions proved "hot". We had a close ad hoc liaison with the Lobos. These were the gunship choppers, a lot of them Huey Cobras, belonging to the Ist Air Cavalry Division and flown by young Warrant Officers who by reputation needed wheel barrows in which to carry their balls around! Their base of operations was also Lai Khe and we had enjoyed a few BBQs reciprocating as hosts. Lobos were often our most available close air support. It was simple as they had given us their "company" VHF FM frequency, so without any command and control channels getting involved we just called "Any Lobo near Grid 123 247, we have a Troops in Contact needing support". It nearly always paid dividends, finding a pair or more of them on their way home still with a handy weapon load. Those young fellows were always spoiling for a fight and quite few LRRPs patrols of the Big Red One are indeed indebted to them.

There was an infuriating routine to the early morning go. Everyone who flew in Vietnam always listened out on GUARD, the UHF frequency specified and reserved solely for use in dire emergency, i.e., in a MAY

DAY situation. Always, but always, someone would hit their transmit button on GUARD and say "Good Morning Vietnam!". OK it was highly illegal and irresponsible to do this but to add to the joy of the moment, someone in an officious, hurt, and commanding voice would find it necessary to reply, "Get off GUARD!". That was just the start. Folk started to get hot under the collar; that person would then have to be told, "Get off Guard, GET OFF GUARD!" and so the unstoppable sequence was under way. The only course open was to switch off GUARD freq until you judged the miscreants had tired of their play.

A regular visual recce mission in the OV-10 at Lai Khe carrying only internal fuel was usually scheduled for two and a half hours, and often lasted three. I was tooling around the AO one morning when the Brigade had the 11th Armoured Cavalry Regiment under operational control. Commanding this Regt was one George S Patton the 3rd, then a Lieutenant Colonel. Interested, and as it was pretty quiet I had tuned to his FM push when I was alarmed by a stream of obscenities and abuse obviously being directed from a CinC chopper to a force on the ground. As I got closer I could see the airborne chopper circling around twin columns of tanks progressing through the bush towards a creek line. The Lt Colonel was intent on getting his tanks to where he had seen some NVA soldiers scurrying into that creek line. On the ground they were not so convinced, particularly as it appeared they were being asked to "dismount" and get after these guys. On the spot Patton relieved one Major of his command and promptly ordered his pilot to land the chopper alongside this creek. I could not believe what I was seeing! But there was more. He jumped out of the aircraft, alone, brandishing the twin pearl handled Colts which he, his pa, and his Grandpappy had always worn, and rushed into the creek scrub line and came out with two prisoners! Whew! I suppose you cannot argue with success, but what an incredibly stupid thing to do. It must have worked though, because I think he eventually made three star rank, but not top of the wozza as had his famous family predecessors. Had I been his commander I would have fired him on the spot. Flg Off Dick Kelloway, RAAF, was a FAC supporting Patton's regiment for while.

A FAC In the TACP at Lai Khe, amongst other notables of course, was one USAF Captain Michael S Poehler, one of the coolest hands and possibly the smoothest pilot I have had the pleasure of sharing a cockpit with. I think he was a self adopted Texan, his family having hailed from much further north. He used to speak of Yankees and "DAMNED YANKEES", the former being northerners who holidayed in Texas, and the others the ones who came to stay. I learned a lot from this gentleman. He had a dice game called "horses" which unendingly cost me a can of beer to his advantage, but I was very pleased to have Mike particularly on a night mission which to-ed and fro-ed for quite a while until the good guys got full control. We flew two up at night because things were a bit more complicated than in daylight. The Brigade was inserting two battalions by helicopter just after dusk to surround, search and destroy enemy, in a nearby village where considerable VC and NVA activity had been emanating. Part of the first landing went as planned. First the Landing Zone (LZ) surrounds were prepared thoroughly with artillery and in this case a couple of pre-planned air strikes. On hand was an AC-47 (Dakota) gunship, a SPOOKY flare ship (another Dakota) both holding above the scene separated at different altitudes. The first wave of troops landed and established themselves but the second wave was opposed strongly despite the pre-landing bombardment. We called up two more sets of fighters (F-100s from Bien Hoa about 5 minutes away) for close air support with snake and nape, and supporting artillery was also committed. Some of the Army slick choppers took some damage. The Spooky was lighting up the place like day with massive parachute flares from higher up. The Puff the Magic Dragon Dakota gunship was laying its unbroken stream of pink tracer mini gun fire. You could hear that gun in the OV-10, starting with a low growl rising to almost a wail as the rate of fire built up. Spectacular stuff against the darkening sky, and coordinating it all was quite an exciting deal. This time it was taking much longer than expected. In the middle of it all the Brigade commander's CinC chopper ran very low on fuel and had to return to Lai Khe for a refill! So, he handed control of the operation to me in the FAC aircraft. I can only speculate what his subordinate commanders on the ground and in the landing process must have thought, but I was absolutely petrified by the idea. Mike in the back seat looked after the fighters, the Spooky and the AC-47 gunship and I chatted with the grunts as necessary for about the 15 -20 minutes the boss took to get back. We got away with it and stayed untouched!

Midyear 1969 Air Commodore Fred Robey (Commander RAAF Vietnam) although not my boss decided I should now go to the Australian Task Force as ALO to apply some of my supposedly fresh close air support knowledge and experience. He convinced his USAF contacts.

So again, there I was at The FACU at Phan Rang. I had to convert to the dreaded O-2 as used by the Jade FACs supporting the Australian Task Force. Dreaded, first because the bloody thing had no stick, and whoever heard of an aircraft without a stick! A yoke was something to use with a draft horse. But not only that the throttles, yeah two of them, were in the middle. If you flew it from the left seat you had to operate throttles, prop pitch, and mixture controls with your right hand that should be reserved for operating the stick and the important things like firing buttons. You had to fly this wretched "wheel" thing with the hand that should be holding the throttle and the press to talk switch. A militarised version of the push-me-pull-ya Cessna 337, the USAF had loaded the O-2 up with radios, put rocket pod hardpoints on both wings, and made some more windows in the doors so the inmates could see out a little better. It finished up heaps over the max all up weight planned by Cessna. With me only in it on a coolish tropical morning out of Vung Tau with full fuel and at full power (not recommended climb power) it would climb at about 350 feet per minute. I never had to try it out in operational circumstances on one engine. I don't think it would have made it home. How did I get here! But there's more. No bang seats and only two five-rocket pods for Willy Petes. My extravagances with WPs like lighting up napalm might have to stop. The few rockets might be sorely needed for target marking. Phuoc Tuy area of operations had quietened considerably by the time I got there so maybe the OV10 values might not be so badly missed in a FAC aircraft. I shudder when I think of the USAF blokes who flew and died in this apology for a FAC aircraft in places like the Trail and on hot SAR missions further north. They were brave, brave men.

At 1ATF we operated based at Vung Tau but flew to the Australian Army base at Nui Dat for briefing and operations. The TACP maintained a radio operating base at Nui Dat. Living at Vung Tau was dangerous because the RAAF officers' mess was too handy, but contact with my own RAAF folk again in No 9 Sqn (choppers) and No 35 Sqn Caribous was helpful re-learning Aussie speak. As it turned out I had seriously converted to US idiom and pronunciation. I had to get people to understand me. My big problem at Nui Dat was that as ALO I was the senior USAF liaison officer but I was walking about in an RAAF flying suit. The ATF fellas never got hold of the idea.

The Aussie Army command had the weird idea that the presence of a FAC aircraft buzzing around the AO was somehow a compromise of their positions and of their intentions. In many cases they preferred us to stay on the ground until needed. The value of FAC visual recce was just not appreciated, nor was the effect on the reaction time of close air support of having a FAC already airborne. The experience was quite by contrast with my time with the Big Red One where I flew almost daily with the commander in his chopper as part of his staff, and ate with him most evenings. At No 1 ATF it took me two weeks to even get to meet the commander, and then it was at an officers' mess function at Nui Dat. I tried, but proper liaison at the top level was never established in my time. At battalion level though, and particularly with No 5 RAR (the Fifth Battalion under Lt Col Colin Kahn) the cooperation was excellent. We did great armed recce work with the Possums (Army light choppers), the RAAF Bushrangers (Chopper gunships), and with the Special Air Service patrols on occasions.

When finally my time was up and I was loaded aboard the Qantas 707 for home, as the aircraft rolled onto the runway at Ton Son Nuht and the captain gave the four jets the power, a great cheer from the crowd on board was quickly curtailed when the power suddenly came off and heavy braking was applied bringing the big jet to a shuddery stop. The captain came on the speakers with the news that he had to abort to miss a light aircraft which had entered the runway ahead of him. All was OK, we had not been taken out on our last day. We just took off about 15 minutes late!

CHAPTER 11

No compilation of Royal Air Force memoirs would be complete without a tale of

The Earl of Bandon c.1950

Paddy Bandon was a pre-war Cranwell graduate who eventually rose to be an Air Chief Marshal. He was impervious to criticism, an irrepressible character who became known as "the abandoned Earl" about whom there are many tales. One that is not generally known took place when he was on the IDC (Imperial Defence College – later Royal College of Defence Studies) course in the late 1940s or early 50s. My stepfather also attended IDC at about the same time.

At the halfway point of the course the students – all very senior officers – were sent off to visit somewhere abroad. Some went to the Far East, some to USA etc. Paddy was made leader of the group of about 15 or 20 sent to visit our occupation forces in Germany. In those days travel was by train to Harwich, ferry boat to Hook of Holland and then another train to destination. I believe their destination was Dusseldorf, but where-ever it was, for some reason they were not met. Paddy decided that hanging about on a platform was not for him; he enquired of the next train out and was shown it standing at the platform. It is said he drew a revolver - but who knows – anyway he went up to the train full of German civilians and ordered them out "RAUS RAUS". Dutifully they obeyed, the IDC group embarked and ever-punctual, the train departed to destinations unknown with a contingent of senior British officers on board as its only passengers. Took a while to sort out, they say.

Thus ends my reminiscing. Again I give thanks to my co-contributors and hope you the reader have enjoyed the stories of the "Old and Bold".

John Daly Canberra May 2016

Printed in Great Britain
by Amazon